Living Faith: Lessons From Abraham

David Watson

Help for the journey...

First published in Great Britain, May 2009
by Gilead Books Publishing
Corner Farm
West Knapton
Malton
North Yorkshire YO17 8JB

www.GileadBooks.com

British Library Cataloguing-in-Publication Data:
A catalogue record for this book is available from the
British Library.

ISBN-13: 978-0-9558099-4-1

The publisher makes every effort to ensure that the
papers used in our books are made from trees that
have been legally sourced from well-managed and
credibly certified forests by using a printer awarded
FSC & PEFC chain of custody certification.

Edited and compiled by Chris Hayes
Cover design by Dave Magill

Mixed Sources
Product group from well-managed
forests, and other controlled sources
www.fsc.org Cert no. TT-COC-002641
© 1996 Forest Stewardship Council
FSC

Foreword

I first heard David Watson preach in 1974 shortly after I had come to faith in Christ. I sat spellbound as I listened to his simple, clear and compelling unravelling of the gospel. I have read every book that he has written — many of them several times.

It is hard to believe that 25 years have passed since David Watson left us. He left behind a rich legacy, one which has continued to impact lives to this day. His preaching introduced many thousands across the globe to a life of faith in Christ, while his many books are still to be found, well-thumbed, on innumerable bookshelves.

The world has changed in so many ways in the last 25 years, yet today, as ever, people still need to hear of the hope a life lived in relationship with God brings; we still need reconciliation and healing in our relationships; the church needs a renewed confidence to engage with the broken world around and to be the missional community it is called to be.

David's teaching was always immensely practical, both in its delivery and its application. His illustrations never distracted but allowed us to enter fully into what the Spirit was saying. His clear simple teaching was always the result of a great gift combined with many hours of study, prayer and preparation. Its application is ever relevant. From time to time we all struggle with disappointment, discouragement and questions of faith. We all need to hear David's calm and confident words, pointing us to the Bible, pointing us to Jesus, helping us on our journey of faith.

I am delighted that through this series of short books, David's teaching will be available not only to those who knew him but to many more people who will find help and comfort through his words.

It is a fact that St Michael le Belfrey church in York where David spent most of his ministry has no memorial to him, no plaque or piece of furniture bearing his name. This is because David's memorial is the fact that a thriving church continues there and the Gospel is still preached. Similarly, this series of books is no "collected works" of David Watson. The desire of those involved is to allow David's teaching to continue to change lives and bring glory to God. This is timeless wisdom for 21st century discipleship and I commend it to you.

Nicky Gumbel
HTB, London
May 2009

Acknowledgements

My thanks go to Anne Watson, Douglas Greenfield and The Belfrey Trust for sharing the desire to see David's teaching available, in written form, to those who never had chance to hear him. To Jeni Farnhill and Roger Simpson for their encouragement along the way. James Harris at Anchor Recordings for making available the recordings. Nick Szkiler and Gilead Music for processing the recordings, and Elisabeth for producing a manuscript from the spoken word. Thanks also to Dave Burton for copy editing and Dave Magill for the cover.

C J Hayes

Contents

Faith in God's promises

A prayer:

> *Heavenly Father, we praise you for the glory and light that you have shone on us down the years; that you have spoken to us in many ways over the centuries, through the Prophets, through the Scriptures and through your last word to us, Jesus Christ. We ask that by your Spirit your word today may become a living word, full of light and truth, bringing to us something fresh of your glory and quickening our faith in you and in your promises. For Jesus Christ's sake. Amen.*

An elderly couple were sitting at home one evening resting after a very hard day's work. He was 75 and a farmer, and she was 66. As a couple, they'd done fairly well at farming and they had many flocks and herds. There was only one special sadness that had been with them all down the years. God had not granted them any children. Now aged 75 and 66 it seemed of course much too late.

I heard the other day that Miss United Kingdom, the beauty queen, visited an old people's home and met a man aged 103! He took one look at this very attractive girl, kissed her gently on the cheek and then sighed and said, "If only I were 10 years younger!"

Well I think, rather like that man, this couple needed to be slightly more than 10 years younger. This man sighed to himself as he sat there and prayed, "Oh Lord, I'm an old man now, and my wife's an old woman. How I wish you had given me a son and heir… but you haven't. So I suppose all my property will go one day to the son of one of my servants."

Then it seemed that God spoke to him very clearly, immediately after that sighed prayer of his. "Your heir will not be your servant or a son of your servant. Your own son shall be your heir."

I don't think he could take it in. It was too mind-boggling even to imagine that it could be true at all. So I think perhaps he said to his wife, "I'll just go out and get some fresh air before turning in tonight. I want some space to think this one through."

He went outside, and probably the sky was cloudless. He looked up at all those myriads of stars shining on him that night, perhaps brighter than he had ever seen them before. Again God seemed quite clearly to speak to him.

"Do you see all those stars? Can you number them? So shall your descendants be."

"Thank you, Lord."

And here's the Bible making its comment about this, because I'm sure you have recognised this as the story of Abraham and Sarah.

> "And [Abraham] believed the LORD, and the LORD counted him as righteous because of his faith." (Genesis 15:6)

Well, the months passed and yet Sarah his wife did not conceive. The months turned into years – one year, two years, three years. Four, five, six, seven, eight years. Nine years, ten years. Nothing happened at all. Had he just imagined that promise? Was it really the word of the Lord or simply his own thoughts and wishes and unfulfilled desires coming into what he felt was God speaking to him? After all, he was now 85, his wife 76. The whole idea was quite ridiculous.

Then Sarah suddenly had a very bright idea (as wives do). Following what was a very normal custom in those days, she said, "Well now, if you had a son by my Egyptian maid Hagar, he would still be your son and he would be your descendant. Perhaps that's what the Lord meant all those years ago. Here we have been waiting for ten years for some kind of miracle to happen. But, of course, if you took my servant as your wife, then it would still be your son. You can have descendants."

"Well, you may be right about that," he said. So Abraham took Hagar as his wife and she bore him a son named Ishmael. Fourteen years later – notice the time interval – 14 years later, God spoke again to Abraham. He was now 99 and Sarah was 90. God said this to Abraham,

> "I will bless [Sarah] and give you a son from her! Yes, I will bless her richly, and she will become the mother of many nations. Kings of nations will be among her descendants." (Genesis 17:16)

Now what would you have said or done if God had said that to you and you were a man of 99 or a woman of 90? Well I'll tell you what Abraham did - and I'm sure perhaps you or I might have done the same. He just laughed! I don't think it was a cynical kind of laugh, a sarcastic laugh, but it seemed just so ridiculous. The Bible says,

> "Then Abraham bowed down to the ground, but he laughed to himself in disbelief." (Genesis 17:17)

Abraham really couldn't believe it at all and said to God,

> "May Ishmael live under your special blessing!" (Genesis 17:18)

"Here's my fine son who is now 14 years old. If only he can live, he'll be my heir. He'll be my descendant, or the first of my descendants."
  God is very gentle and gracious with him because Abraham is not mocking God at all. He just finds it hard to accept, and God said,

> "No-Sarah, your wife, will give birth to a son for you. You will name him Isaac (meaning "he laughs") and I will confirm my covenant with him and his descendants as an everlasting covenant." (Genesis 17:19)

Now, that's astonishing. Abraham believed that promise of God. Within a year it all happened. Sarah miraculously conceived. The pregnancy went well, and Isaac was born.

Notice again – let me stress this point – that God's promise was fulfilled 24 years after it had first been given. I think some of us are a little impatient when we are waiting for God to answer our prayers or fulfil his promises. In an age of instant coffee and instant whip and instant mash and instant news, and instant photographs, we want instant answers to our faith and prayers. We want to see it happening at once. Well, Abraham waited for 24 years. Therefore Abraham's faith is held up to us in the New Testament as the supreme example of faith, the model of faith, that we need today in order to receive the blessings of God, even the most basic blessings of God, of his acceptance and forgiveness.

So we read from Romans 4 verses 20-21, where Paul says this:

> *"Abraham never wavered in believing God's promise. In fact, his faith grew stronger, and in this he brought glory to God. He was fully convinced that God is able to do whatever he promises."*

Because of Abraham's faith, God *"counted him as righteous"*. But these words were not written for his sake alone, but for ours also. In other words, here's the faith that you and I should have, faith particularly in the God who raised Jesus from the dead.

So what is faith? It's taking God at his word; acting on his promise or word; trust. Basically, belief - in everyday terms, in ordinary relationships - is trusting a person, trusting the promise of that person, trusting the word of that person. Taking them, if you like, at their word. It's the basis of all relationships. As I have often said in evangelistic services, if you say something to me, and I don't believe you, I don't trust you, it is impossible for us to have a relationship.

The very first step in all relationships on a human level, let alone between man and God, is that we must take each other at each other's word. So it is that we come to God by faith. As the writer to the Hebrews said,

> *"And it is impossible to please God without faith. Anyone who wants to come to him must believe that God exists and that he rewards those who sincerely seek him." (Hebrews 11:6)*

Faith is the essence of every relationship.

We are looking at faith in God's promises. With Abraham there were three stages that I think are most important for us today. First of all, Abraham <u>knew</u> the promise of God. God said to him, *"you will have a son of your own who will be your heir." (Genesis 15:4)* And even though after 10 years he listened to Sarah's bright idea, he never really doubted the promise of God. He knew what God had said.

I am told on fairly good authority that there are something like 17,000 promises in the Bible. But with any promise of God we need to ask two simple questions.

First, does that promise apply to me or to us in our situation today? Just to give an example, when Jesus said on one occasion, to one particular individual, *"Your faith has made you well" (Luke 8:48)* we can't therefore apply that particular promise to every single time we are sick and say to ourselves, "Well, if I have faith I shall be well". It's not always as straightforward as that. No more should we take that simple particular word that Jesus said to the Rich Young Ruler *"Sell all your possessions and give the money to the poor" (Matthew 19:21)* and apply it to all of us in every situation. Basically, these are particular words to particular people for particular occasions. Sometimes the Spirit may light them up to us and make them a very personal word again to us – I've often found that to be true – but we've got to be sure that a promise we read in the Bible can legitimately apply to us in our situation here and now.

Of course there are hundreds and hundreds of promises in the Bible about which we can be totally sure and quite convinced that God means what he says: the assurance and promise that God loves us, just as we are; that he washes away all our sins as we come to him; that he longs to fill our lives day by day with his Holy Spirit, fill our

15

lives with his love; that in everything he works for good; that he will meet all our needs; that one day we shall be with him forever in his home in heaven. These are the sort of promises we know apply to us. There are many, many others like them. Anyway, first question: does that promise really apply?

Second question: are the conditions fulfilled? Because most of God's promises have clear conditions attached to them. For example, the Bible says that if we confess our sins, then God will forgive us and cleanse us from all unrighteousness. (1 John 1:9) But we've got to confess, we've got to repent of our sins first of all. If we seek first the Kingdom of God and his righteousness, all these things that we are worrying about will be added unto us. God will meet every need of ours providing we seek him first – his kingdom, his righteousness. And so on.

It is impossible to have faith without obedience. Obedience is the key which opens the door to God's will and promises. If God is not fulfilling his promises, it is probably because of disobedience – in our hearts or somewhere in our community. We need to remember that sometimes he tests our faith by allowing a gap. It may be even 24 years before the promise is fulfilled.

One delightful illustration of faith comes from the Newcastle City Hall where, together with various teams, I've been privileged to lead festivals of praise over the last few years. Whilst the team is rehearsing on the stage before the festival, I wait in the conductor's room. Just off this room there's a toilet which is the most unusual toilet I think I have ever been into! There is no window or anything of any kind to let in the light. There is no light whatsoever. There is a bulb, very high up, indicating a promise of light, but no indication whatsoever of how that promise can be fulfilled.

What you have to do is act in faith, just in sheer blind faith. You have to go into that loo and shut the door. As soon as you lock the door, at that moment, the light comes on. To begin with I wasn't prepared to lock the door until the light had come on, but nothing happened! Once I had locked the door then all was well.

Now that's an illustration of faith. You have to act, you have to obey the promise before it is actually fulfilled. It is interesting that Peter in his second letter talks about the tremendous promises that God has given us, his great and precious promises, through which you escape from the corruption that is in the world through lust and become partakers of the divine nature.

Because God has given you these promises, everything you could ever need is there in Christ. All the promises are there to assure you.

"In view of all this, make every effort to respond to God's promises. Supplement your faith with a generous provision of moral excellence, and moral excellence with knowledge, and knowledge with self-control, and self-control with patient endurance, and patient endurance with godliness, and godliness with

brotherly affection, and brotherly affection with love for everyone. The more you grow like this, the more productive and useful you will be in your knowledge of our Lord Jesus Christ." (2 Peter 1:5-8)

In other words, faith by itself is not enough. Faith without works is dead. There must be obedience and the fulfilment of certain conditions before we see the blessings of these precious and very great promises.

John Calvin often used to say while it is faith alone that justifies, faith that justifies is never alone. Always it is accompanied with obedience and some evidence of that faith. So does the promise apply? Are the conditions fulfilled? Abraham knew the promise of God. Secondly he believed the promise of God.

> *"Abraham never wavered in believing God's promise." (Romans 4:20)*

If you look at verse 18 – I love the way Paul puts it here – *"Even when there was no reason for hope, Abraham kept hoping."* Now that is real faith – hoping against hope. In fact faith begins only when we have run out of answers ourselves, only when we have come to an end of our wisdom, our strength, our resources. When my toe is on the bottom of the swimming bath I am not swimming. It's only when I am completely out of my depth that I have to swim. Otherwise I sink completely.

Therefore God will bring us into situations, both personally and as a fellowship, when we are totally out of our depth, when we have no answers; we have run out of our resources. We have come to a full stop. We simply have to trust God and God's promises to us. Without him, we are without hope. If there is no God, there are no answers. But, said Jesus, *"with God everything is possible"* *(Matthew 19:26)*. Here at the end of Romans 4 verse 17, Paul speaks of

> *"God who brings the dead back to life and who creates new things out of nothing."*

All things are possible with God, of course - he is omnipotent! And, said Jesus, *"Anything is possible if a person believes." (Mark 9:23)*

Now we may know the promises of God, that's good. But God will allow difficulties and pains in our experiences so that we have to believe in him and in his promises. Otherwise it is quite hopeless: we sink.

So let's say we have a crisis, maybe with our financial situation, or crisis with our job or crisis in our home or church. Wherever it may be and whatever the crisis, there seems to be no solution, a totally impossible situation. At that moment – and very likely <u>only</u> at that moment – faith can step in. We have to believe God. We have to trust the one who gives life to the dead. There is nothing else that we can do. Someone has said "Doubt has two arguments: 'Will God do this?' and 'Can God do this?'" Nagging questions. But faith has two arguments also: God will do it because he has promised; and God can do it because he is omnipotent. Faith means being certain of things we cannot see. Therefore again,

> *"Abraham never wavered in believing God's promise. In fact, his faith grew stronger, and in this he brought glory to God. He was fully convinced that God is able to do whatever he promises." (Romans 4:20,21)*

Now we may know all this in our heads, but we need to prove it in our own lives too. We prove it in our own lives only perhaps when we really have to. So faith is not blind optimism, it's not wishful thinking, it's not pious dreams. It's not even knowing the promises of God. It's total realism – facing realistically the facts of the situation together with the facts of God's promises, which may seem to be completely opposite at the time. Hoping against hope.

  We see death, but believe that God gives us eternal life. We see sin, but believe God can wash away all our sin and accepts us just as we are in Jesus Christ. We see chaos but believe the promise that the Lord reigns. We see many things which make us sad and depressed, <u>but</u> we look at the promise of God and our faith rises. Now that is faith. Abraham knew the promise of God. He believed it also to be true in spite of everything.

Thirdly and lastly, Abraham praised God that this promise was true. Notice verse 20.

> *"Abraham never wavered in believing God's promise. In fact, his faith grew stronger, and in this he brought glory to God."*

The tense of that in Greek is really this: he grew strong in his faith as he went <u>on and on</u> giving glory to God. Remember he had to go on and on praising and waiting for 24 years before that promise was fulfilled.

Many of the examples of faith given to us in the Scriptures and in the history of the church right up to the present day are very similar — long, waiting, testing times. Joseph had his great dreams, but it was 13 years before they were fulfilled - in prison for 13 years. In more recent times Richard Wurmbrand[1] was 14 years in prison. These precious and very great promises are not fulfilled overnight.

God's delays test not only our faith but also our love. When you love someone very much, really love them and not lust after them, you're willing to wait for them. As you wait for them, so that love for them can grow and grow and grow, providing you are positive and full of faith in your waiting. That's why Abraham's example is so important for

---

[1] Romanian pastor, imprisoned for opposing the state church of the Communist regime. Lived 1909-2001.

us. He grew strong in his faith as he went on giving glory to God. The question for us really is, in which direction are we looking when God has put us in at the deep end and we simply have to trust him? Do we look at our problems and get more and more filled with anxieties and worries and fears, or become critical of those who may in some part have caused our problems? Or do we look at God in all his greatness and faithfulness and love, wisdom and understanding? Do we praise him for all these things? Because as we praise him, then our problems get into the right perspective. Our faith will grow and our love will grow too.

We know in this church at the moment there are various difficulties we are facing. We need to be realistic about it. We know too that in recent months God has really seriously challenged us about our love for him, that we have lost something of our first love.

Now what are we to do? Get discouraged, become critical, cynical? No, according to this picture of Abraham, we are to take the promises of God that we know apply to us in this and other situations, fulfilling the conditions, especially obedience. Believe those promises to be true in spite of everything, hoping against hope, and then go on praising God that he is true, that his word is true, that he never breaks his word, even if we have to wait some time for the real fulfilment of that word. But in this way, not only will our faith grow but our love also will grow for him. Now on top of all that we will see God's blessings on us and through us as we have never seen them before.

"Do you see those stars that there were in the night sky? Can you number them?" So shall your blessings be if you have faith, real faith, based upon the word of God and expressed in worship and praise and obedience. If as you read this, you laugh, you have good patriarchal precedence – Abraham laughed. If at this moment you feel as if he has thrown you right into the deep end, hopelessly out of your depth, remember it is only because he longs for you to swim in the ocean of his love. God knows what he is doing. His love for us will never, never fail. It's all around us, above us, underneath us, everywhere, always working for our good. He simply waits for us to trust him and to praise him. But it is always true.

Let us pray:
Just take a moment to reflect upon that wonderful picture of Abraham trusting God's promises. May be there is a real anxiety in your mind or heart at this moment about something, or it's been there for some time. Realise that in his love, God who works in everything for our good is simply saying to you or to me "You don't know the answer, do you? Well now, look up and trust me. Trust my promises. Learn to swim in the ocean of my love. I'll never fail you."

Father we thank you that your love is higher and greater, richer and more wonderful than anything any of us can imagine. Forgive us for the many times that we are prepared to trust only when we can understand how a situation can be solved. Give us faith in you, a living faith, when we run out of our own resources.

Help us in any area where perhaps at this moment we are defeated or fearful, anxious about tomorrow, to trust you, and not only to trust you but to express our faith with real worship, praise and rejoicing from our hearts, that in your perfect timing as you see our faith grow and our love grow through praise, through giving you glory you may be able to fulfil that promise in your word. We trust you Lord for this. Thank you in Jesus' name. Amen.

Faith in the darkest moments

"Now Sarai, Abram's[2] wife, had not been able to bear children for him." (Genesis 16:1)

This was very clearly a moment of severe testing for Abraham and Sarah. Some time ago in chapter 15 God had given them both a wonderful promise. Abraham had gone outside his tent one night, looked up to the starry sky to see all those million points of light that were sprinkled across the heavens. As he looked up at that wonderfully beautiful scene, God said to him, "Do you see all those stars, Abraham? Can you count them? Can you possibly number them? Your descendants will be as many as those." We're told that Abraham believed the Lord.

I don't know if he had any sleep that night, because it was a marvellous promise to him and his wife. They were childless and they were old people. Certainly I'm sure he was terribly excited as he broke the news at breakfast next morning to his wife. No doubt they went aside and praised the Lord and sang to him for this tremendous gift.

However, a year passed by, and there was no sign of any child. Two years passed by and still no sign. Three years. Four years. Five, six, seven, eight. Nine years, ten years passed by. Still not any

---

[2] After their covenant with God in Genesis 17, Sarai and Abram changed their names to Sarah and Abraham, see page 43.

sign of a child whatsoever. I'm quite sure they might have thought to themselves "Well, perhaps it was all a dream. I mean, maybe it was just Abraham's imagination. They had been longing for this, so he thought that God had said this to him. But of course perhaps it wasn't right at all."

Ten years is a long time. I know some of you have been trusting the promise of God for some specific thing for two or three years. And you know how long that seems. You know the need of patience. The Bible says you have need of patience if you are going to receive what he has promised. Certainly there is tremendous need of patience in the realm of faith. It has been said that there are two sorts of Christians: those who really believe, and those who believe that they believe. You usually can't tell the difference between them until it comes to the test: maybe disappointment, maybe unanswered prayer, maybe hardship, maybe persecution. When it comes to the test, then you will know who really believes and who only believes that they believe.

Undoubtedly God in his wisdom allows tests like this so that we might know what sort of believer we really are. Perhaps you have been praying for guidance, maybe guidance concerning God's great plan for your life, where he is going to lead you and direct you. Maybe guidance concerning marriage or a job, and you have no answer at all. God is completely silent. Maybe you've been praying about a "thorn in the flesh", some affliction, some weakness. You've been praying, perhaps several times, but with absolutely no answer at all. Paul himself had to pray earnestly three times before God gave him an answer. Maybe you've been praying about some illness, some sickness of one kind or another. Perhaps there's a promise that you've felt God has given you some years ago. You've gone on now for years and there is no change whatsoever. Perhaps you have been praying for years for the conversion of a friend or relative, maybe a husband, or children, maybe parents. You've gone on year after year and God is quite silent. The heavens are as brass. There's no change, there's no progress, there's no conviction, or anything. It may have been for ten years. It's a long time, a real test of faith.

It's rightly said that once you launch out into faith, there are going to be a lot of problems. Maybe this is because when you launch out in faith, many people are afraid of what will happen if nothing happens. A woman was travelling on an RAF plane during the war and a sergeant had explained to her how to use the parachute that was strapped around her. And she asked the very relevant question, "What happens if I am halfway down and I pull the ring and nothing happens?" "Oh," he said, "it's quite straightforward; you take it back to the government and make a complaint."

But I think that's a fair question, because what happens if I launch out in faith? The essence of faith is that we do something before we know that the thing is going to work. That is the whole meaning of faith. In the Christian realm it means that we must trust utterly God's faithfulness. We must base our lives, maybe the whole of our lives on his promise, our hopes upon his promise. Indeed God's word and his promises are the same. They will always stand forever; they cannot be broken.

The whole of the life of faith, from conversion to heaven, has this potential trust in God's faithfulness. How does a person find Christ? Well, the way you find Christ is by claiming simply a promise of the Lord Jesus: Revelation 3 verse 20, which says that if we ask him to come into our hearts he will come in. That's the way you begin, by trusting his faithfulness to his own promise. How do you deal with the Holy Spirit? It's the same thing - because Jesus promised that God gives the Holy Spirit to those who ask him. How do you find victory over temptation and sin? You trust, you claim the simple promises of God. It's always the same thing. This is the essence of the Christian faith: trusting the faithfulness of God. That is why God will test us, because he wants to strengthen our faith.

Richard Wurmbrand, whose faith was tested for 14 years in a communist prison, said this about faith. "Faith can be put in two words – 'though' and 'yet'." In the book of Job we read,

> "*Though* He slay me, *yet* will I hope in him." (Job 13:15, NIV)

Many times these words come together in the Bible. They tell us to have faith in the darkest moments. I wonder if you can say that about your own relationship with God, through Christ? <u>Though</u> this may happen, <u>yet</u> I will trust him. <u>Though</u> my prayer seems to be unanswered, <u>yet</u> I will trust him. <u>Though</u> I may have fantastic disappointments in the future, <u>yet</u> I will trust him. That is the essence of faith.

Well, this was a dark moment in the lives of Abraham and Sarah. In their training in faith they had not quite come to the point where they could say confidently "though" and "yet". There were two obstacles, which are common obstacles in the life of faith: the mind and the heart.

First of all, the mind. Perhaps more of a problem for some than for others. We don't know for certain that this was a problem for Abraham and Sarah, but I'm pretty sure it was. You see, God's promise was now 10 years old. Abraham was now 86, and Sarah 76. In human terms there was no possibility whatsoever that a child could now be born. In point of fact they had to wait another 14 years - Abraham 100, Sarah 90 – before anything happened. But of course miracles like this today would seem to us even more fantastic and incredible than they might have done to Abraham and Sarah.

I think I want to pause at this for a moment because all of us, including Christians, probably far more than we realise, have been affected by the materialistic outlook of this age. We can believe things that we understand, or at any rate that could be understood in scientific terms. But we find it very hard to believe something that we cannot understand. We say it can't happen because we can't understand it, or there is no possible explanation for it. That's why I think with a genuine desire to reach across to scientists and humanists, John A.T. Robinson wrote the book "But That I Can't Believe". In the book he explains what he can't believe in the Christian faith, and how he can't believe in the supernatural elements. These are some of the chapter headings: Adam and Eve, Virgin Birth, Miracles, Resurrection, The Second Coming, and Hell. There are many, many Christians, professing Christians, who would say, "but that, I can't believe. It's supernatural – I can't take it."

I doubt if we realise what a sacred cow science has become. We believe the laws of science; we don't always believe the laws of God: that he is our creator, that he is our sustainer, that with him all things are possible. It is interesting to note how few Christian leaders, that I personally know and admire, really believe in the truth of divine healing. You see, when it comes to God giving a person peace, we can understand that - because you and I could almost give that person peace, if we had enough time, patience and love. But when it comes to God healing broken bones or curing someone of cancer, that's rather different.

When it comes to church finances, you find that churches try all sorts of worldly means, because they don't understand how or they don't believe that God can really answer prayer as far as the material things are concerned. I know of one church which had to find £30,000 to build a new building. What did they do? Did they rush round with collecting boxes and rob all the houses in the parish? No, the congregation prayed for a whole week. They set aside as much time as possible, so that for a whole week there was continuous prayer going up from the congregation. £30,000 came within four months. There are many examples like that. It's significant that when John the Baptist was having doubts about Jesus Christ, that Jesus sent these credentials back to John. He said,

> *"Go back to John and tell him what you have heard and seen - the blind see, the lame walk, the lepers are cured, the deaf hear, the dead are raised to life, and the Good News is being preached to the poor." (Matthew 11:4,5)*

It is sheer arrogance if I doubt some promise of God because I don't understand it. This is reducing Almighty God to the size of my own mind. It is no wonder that God says very strongly to the prophet Isaiah,

> *"My thoughts are nothing like your thoughts," says the Lord. "And my ways are far beyond anything you could imagine. For just as the heavens are higher than the earth, so my ways*

*are higher than your ways and my thoughts
higher than your thoughts." (Isaiah 55:8,9)*

Of course, the finite creature cannot begin to comprehend the infinite creator.

So, the mind is the first common obstacle to faith which probably most of us would confess to being hindered by. Any of you with a particular scientific mind or who are nurses or doctors, or anyone who is involved in some scientific line, I have every sympathy with you, for at times you find it very hard to see how God could do this or that or the other. But he is Almighty God.

The second obstacle to faith is the heart. At any rate it was so for Abraham and Sarah.

> *"Now Sarai, Abram's wife, had not been able to bear children for him. But she had an Egyptian servant named Hagar. So Sarai said to Abram, "The LORD has prevented me from having children. Go and sleep with my servant. Perhaps I can have children through her."* (Genesis 16:1,2)

It seems amazing to us that it was a local custom that if the wife of a man could not bear children, then sometimes the husband might seek to have children by a maidservant. So that any child born would still become in some measure the child of that family. Well, of course God never suggested this to Abraham and Sarah. He had promised them a child of their own. But you can understand what was going on in the hearts of Abraham and Sarah at this point. After ten years, nothing had happened.

Therefore Sarah, longing for a child that she could call her own, longing that there should be some child to be an heir to the family, and seeing there was no hope, simply did what a lot of her pagan friends and neighbours did quite often, and took a familiar pagan custom and suggested this to Abraham. She must have known this wasn't the best way forward. But you see her emotions, her feelings, her longings and her yearnings were dominating her thoughts. This is a very dangerous position to be in. She made this suggestion to Abraham, and Abraham, knowing how depressed and disappointed she was because she was childless, hadn't the courage of his convictions to say no. Therefore we read these words at the end of verse 2,

> "Abraham listened to the voice of Sarai." (NASB)

Up to now he had always listened to the voice of the Lord. It wasn't always easy but when he listened, there was blessing. Now his heart became a stumbling block to his faith. Out of human sympathy and affection and kindness – human love – we are told that he listened to the voice of Sarah. Friendship and love between human beings is a very wonderful thing, especially of course between husband and wife. But Christ knew very well what he was saying when he said these chilling words,

> *"Your enemies will be right in your own household! If you love your father or mother more than you love me, you are not worthy of being mine; or if you love your son or daughter more than me, you are not worthy of being mine." (Matthew 10: 36,37)*

And we could add – "husband, wife, boyfriend, girlfriend - anyone - more than me", said Jesus, "is not worthy of being mine". And we may often find that if we are really loving Jesus most of all, there will be times within our circle of friends and relatives, when we will not be popular or understood, and even severely criticised for what we are doing. "That's selfish, that's ungrateful!" Many a Christian has suffered like that in his or her home. It's interesting how Mary, who after all loved Jesus her own son, when she made a suggestion to Jesus at a wedding, heard this reply,

> *"Woman, what does your concern have to do with Me? My hour has not yet come." (John 2:4, NKJV)*

And Peter who loved Jesus, when he tried to suggest that Jesus should not go forward to death, heard this stinging rebuke,

"Get behind Me, Satan". (Matthew 16:23)

From time to time, a person's enemies will be those of their own family and circle of friends. And if your heart controls your actions, then quite certainly you will find that you will be led away from Jesus Christ sometimes. Without any question at all it will hinder your faith.

I've just had great blessing on holiday reading the story of John Sung, a great Chinese evangelist. And it was interesting how this man who led so many hundreds of thousands to Christ in quite a short lifetime, had no small talk. He couldn't comment on the weather – or whatever people comment on in China. He lacked all the social graces. He couldn't spend time with the rather longwinded Chinese customs. He appeared at times to be abrupt and rude. Why? Because he had only one ambition and that was to please God. If people were half as anxious to please God as they are to please other people, there would be countless red-hot Christians everywhere.

Well, after a moment's weakness and hesitation, Abraham listened to Sarah when she was depressed. Just in passing, it is always a very great mistake to make an important decision when you or someone else is depressed. You will never make the right decision. But Abraham and Sarah made a decision when she was depressed. They realised later how wrong they had been. Their action brought many sorrows with it: sorrows for Abraham who went against his convictions and conscience and acted in unbelief; sorrows for Hagar who, after the birth of her child, was despised by Sarah; she despised Sarah herself and was cast out into the wilderness; sorrows too for Sarah who was filled with jealousy and bitterness and had to wait 14 years for the birth of her own child; and of course sorrows for God as he saw that Abraham and Sarah had failed in this test. There always is sorrow when you fail to follow the Lord wholeheartedly. I know it in my own heart. As a minister and pastor I have seen sorrow in congregations because people are listening to the voice of someone else or following their own wishes or desires, their own mind or heart, anything but listening to the voice of the Lord.

However as a final encouraging word in this episode of Abraham and Sarah, I want you to notice God's overruling mercy and grace. In the New Testament this particular story in Genesis 16 is taken up by Paul as a wonderful allegory or illustration of the two great covenants of God. (Galatians 4:21-31)

This story describes a wrong turning, a wrong move by Abraham and Sarah. Yet in the New Testament, they are held up as the supreme example of faith, never of failure. Always God has seen their sins and forgiven them for that. Always they are seen as an example of faith. As Paul says,

> *"And Abraham's faith did not weaken, even*
> *though, at about 100 years of age, he figured*
> *his body was as good as dead—and so was*

36

Sarah's womb. Abraham never wavered in believing God's promise. In fact, his faith grew stronger, and in this he brought glory to God. He was fully convinced that God is able to do whatever he promises." (Romans 4:19-21)

Now I want you to notice those words *"His faith grew stronger."* Faith is a living thing. It has to grow, and it has to grow strong. And it does so as you start praising God for his promises. He will test you, right enough. You may fail. But as you go on praising him, as you go on learning from your mistakes, as you go on trusting him and his faithfulness, you will prove in your own experience that he is indeed utterly faithful, that he is always able to do what he has promised, whatever your mind or your heart may think or feel.

Let us pray:

It may be that you have a battle in your heart at the moment. God has shown you the way that you ought to go. But either you can't understand it, you can't believe it, or else your heart is deceiving you. Maybe your affection for someone else is spoiling your affection for the Lord. Just commit that matter to God's hands now. He knows your problems. He longs to bless with his fullest blessing.

Heavenly Father, we thank you with all our hearts that you have given all of us so many great promises in your word. We thank you that they have been proved down the centuries, and always you have been found to be utterly faithful to your word. Forgive us that sometimes we doubt you. Forgive us that sometimes we hearken to the voice of another. Help us to feed upon your word and upon the living Lord Jesus, so to praise and glorify your name so that our faith also may grow strong, fully convinced that you can do what you've promised. We ask it for Jesus Christ's sake. Amen.

Waiting for the promise

"When Abram was 99 years old, the Lord appeared to him." (Genesis 17:1)

A man by the name of John Newton Baker once made this very shrewd remark: You can measure a person by the size of the things that make them mad. In other words, if someone loses their patience over little things, they are "little". On the other hand, if they remain patient over great things, they are "great".

By all measurement quite clearly Abraham was a great man, because when Abraham was 99 years old, the Lord appeared to him. I'm not saying that this was the first time that the Lord appeared to him, certainly not, but it seems to be the first significant time for 24 years. 24 years previously, God had promised Abraham that he would have the gift of a son, of his own son Isaac. Ten years passed, nothing happened. Then Abraham had a son by Sarah's maidservant Hagar, and they called his name Ishmael. God was still silent. No sign whatsoever of the original promise being fulfilled. It went on like this for another 14 years. 24 years altogether. Abraham was very patient indeed. I would say he was a great man because of this, even though he had that temporary lapse part way through. Eventually, when Abraham was 99 years old, the Lord appeared.

Because Abraham was patient, God gave him three new outstanding gifts: first of all, a new revelation of his nature. You see, when the Lord appeared to Abraham in verse one, he said to him, *"I am El-Shaddai—'God Almighty.' Serve me faithfully and live a blameless life."* In other words, "Abraham, do you remember that promise I gave you all those years ago? By now I expect you feel that it is not going to happen, that it's too late perhaps. Well look, Abraham, I am going to reveal something about my character and nature that you may not have realised until now. I'm going to tell you what sort of God I really am. Abraham, listen carefully. I am God Almighty. I am God All-Powerful. I am the sort of God, Abraham, for whom nothing is impossible, nothing is too hard. And what's more, Abraham, that promise I gave you all those years ago will never, never be broken." He went on in verse 2 to say, *"I will make a covenant with you, by which I will guarantee to give you countless descendants."* Abraham, overawed by this new revelation of God − he hadn't seen it quite like this before, this great mountain of the glory of his God − simply fell down and worshipped.

Now here's a typical example of the graciousness of our God. If you wait patiently for him, maybe through some time of testing, not understanding what he is doing or why, but waiting for a new revelation of him, so you might know more of him and his reality, then quite certainly he will give you a new insight. It will be insight into his ways, into his character, into his faithfulness, into his power. It will be quite different from an intellectual understanding of the doctrine. It will be a real insight so that you know it's true and are able to live in the light of it.

You may suddenly realise, for example, that Christ is a living person to be found here and now. You may suddenly realise that the power of the Spirit is available to all those that believe. You may suddenly realise that God is your heavenly father. And concerning that particular problem you've got, he knows all about it, he cares. All things work together for good to those that love God. (Romans 8:28) Or you may suddenly realise, as Abraham did here, that God is Almighty. Another verse in Psalm 70 where it says this is,

> *"May those who love your salvation repeatedly shout, "God is great!" (Psalm 70:4)*

I remember a prayer time about two years ago, where we had a visit from a very fine Nigerian Christian, who had gone back to his own country as a missionary; and he prayed a wonderful prayer. It seemed a real Spirit-inspired prayer. At one point he almost took off, declaring, "God, you're great, you're great, you're great." Our faith simply rose as we began to realise in the Spirit how great our God was. And from that moment on in the prayer meeting we had a new insight into God's greatness, into his power, and new faith with which to believe it. Our prayer went on with a new boldness and courage. That's why I never tire of being with others in fellowship. Because faith is infectious. It's like a glorious disease. If you get in close touch with others who have this disease, you might catch it yourself.

It says in Daniel that those who know their God will be strong and do exploits, because they can see how great God is. Because God is a living God, quite certainly he will reveal himself to you again and again if you are looking for more of him. He will do it constantly. In small ways he should do it every single day if you wait upon him and read your Bible prayerfully. In the East African Revival, Christians regularly asked one another as they passed each other by "What has the Lord shown you today? What has the Lord told you today?" Now, I am not suggesting that we should copy them and do it just automatically like this, but what if I were to ask you "What has the Lord told you today as you read your Bible?" Of course, if you haven't opened your Bible, you've only yourself to blame if the Lord tells you nothing. But if we come patiently, waiting, seeking, looking, praying, then God will reveal himself more and more - more and more of his ways and workings, his power, his faithfulness. Although of course tremendous revelation like Abraham had here, which may change the whole course of our life, will obviously be rarer.

Secondly, in this new revelation of himself, God gave Abraham the assurance of a new relationship with him. Verse 4 in chapter 17,

"This is my covenant with you: I will make you the father of a multitude of nations! What's more, I am changing your name. It will no longer be Abram. Instead, you will be called Abraham, for you will be the father of many nations..."

Abram to Abraham — not very significant you may feel. "What's in a name?" asked Juliet once when she was on the balcony, trying to console her beloved Romeo. "What's in a name? That which we call a rose by any other name would smell as sweet." Now does it really matter if I'm called Tom, Dick or Harry? Does it really matter if it is Abram or Abraham? In the Bible, yes. Because in those days a name always stood for a person's character or nature. For instance, God always revealed himself by a name. He called himself for example Jehovah Jireh, meaning "The Lord will provide". He called himself Jehovah Rapha, "the Lord who heals", Jehovah Shammah "the Lord is there", Jehovah Ra-ha "the Lord is my shepherd", El Shaddai "God Almighty" — all different aspects of God's character.

Jesus came into the world and said *"I am the Bread of Life"*, *"I am the Good Shepherd"*, *"I am..."* this that and the other. Throughout the Bible, wherever men and women came into a new relationship with God they were often given a new name to signify that new relationship, that new nature. Jacob, meaning "deceiver", was given the new name Israel, meaning "prince with God".

Simon, was given the new name Peter, meaning "rock". Certainly he was the rock of the Christian church after Pentecost.

In the same way we talk about a "Christian name", literally the name that we ought to get when we become Christians. Sadly though, in this country the whole thing has got confused because we are still living as though this were a Christian country. Of course it's not, but in a mission setting, in other countries, when a person is converted and baptised they are sometimes given literally a "Christian name".

I rather wish this practice were brought back into this country because at present, we can forget the tremendous change in a person's life when they come to Jesus. They are a totally new creation. They have a new relationship with God. They are born again, born into God's family. They have a new nature, a new life. Something totally new. Therefore what could be better than to give them a new name? Just as a woman when she marries changes from her maiden name to a married name, a reminder of a new and permanent relationship. No longer Anne McEwan-Smith but Anne Watson – for better for worse, for richer for poorer. She may find it takes a bit of time to get used to it, but she will in the long run. I often wonder incidentally why it is that the man doesn't have to change his name as well, but perhaps there's a theological reason for that.

God sealed his new covenant relationship with Abraham and Sarah by giving them a new name.

The change in the name is very interesting. Not Abram, meaning "exalted father", but Abraham, meaning "father of a great multitude". So when Abraham came into a new relationship with God two things happened. He was no longer exalted – "Abram". He might well have said "now it is not I but God" just as Paul said later *"not I but Christ"*. He was now no longer exalted in his life; God was exalted. God was now at the centre.

The other change that happened was he would now be a blessing to other people, the father of a great multitude. When you come to a new relationship with God, God is longing to use you to be a blessing to others. In a sense, that's why he gave this new name to Abraham, showing him that he would be a blessing to many, many people to come.

Sarai means "fighter" or "struggler"; Sarah means "princess" or "queen". Again what a spiritual picture we have of the new relationship: no longer fighting or struggling to earn God's favour but now a princess, someone who is an heir of God, someone who can enjoy all the riches of God's palace.

A new name...I wonder if you have come into this new personal relationship with God. What name would best describe the new life that God has given you, the new purpose that God has for you? Are you sure about this new life in Christ? I've talked practically every week to people who are not sure about it. Do you know that your life is linked with God, that you have found the right way? Do you? Because if you are not 100% sure I do hope that you will take the opportunity to talk to someone about this. It is so important to have a real relationship with God, to have this new life which he longs for you to have.

So Abraham received a new <u>revelation</u> of God, and a new <u>relationship</u> with God. And thirdly, a new <u>rejoicing</u> in God. And here I think is the most delightful sequel to this story.

> *"Then God said to Abraham, 'Regarding Sarai, your wife—her name will no longer be Sarai. From now on her name will be Sarah. And I will bless her and give you a son from her! Yes, I will bless her richly, and she will become the mother of many nations. Kings of nations will be among her descendants.' Then Abraham bowed down to the ground, but he laughed to himself in disbelief. 'How could I become a father at the age of 100?' he thought. 'And how can Sarah have a baby when she is ninety years old?'" (Genesis 17:15-17)*

At first sight I thought it was probably laughter because Abraham just didn't believe. "Why, how ridiculous!" In the same way, if you have your Bible and turn over a page to chapter 18, Sarah also laughed (verses 12-14).

> *"So she laughed silently to herself and said, 'How could a worn-out woman like me enjoy*

> such pleasure, especially when my master—my husband—is also so old?' Then the LORD said to Abraham, 'Why did Sarah laugh? Why did she say, 'Can an old woman like me have a baby?' Is anything too hard for the LORD? I will return about this time next year, and Sarah will have a son'"

Interesting that here the Lord rebuked Sarah, "Why did you laugh? Don't you believe me?" However, it's possible of course to laugh in God's presence because you're so happy. If you turn to Genesis chapter 21 you'll see here an occasion where Sarah laughed because she was so happy because in her old age Isaac had been born to her.

> "'God has brought me laughter. All who hear about this will laugh with me. Who would have said to Abraham that Sarah would nurse a baby? Yet I have given Abraham a son in his old age!" (Genesis 21:6,7).

She was absolutely bubbling over. She couldn't help it – she was so happy. I believe this is the right interpretation of our passage in chapter 17, "then Abraham bowed down to the ground." He laughed with joy and happiness, and said, "How could I become a father at the age of 100?" He could scarcely believe it - but he did believe it. And therefore he just rejoiced and laughed and praised. Certainly God didn't rebuke him here. In fact, God went further and called the promised child Isaac

47

which means "laughter" in memory of Abraham's laughter when he believed the Lord, as the Lord encouraged him. "You see," the Lord said to him, "I haven't forgotten you. I haven't forgotten my promise." As Abraham believed again, so he laughed and praised.

The Bible quite often speaks about this kind of laughter and joy and praise. One of my favourite psalms is Psalm 126.

> *"When the LORD brought back his exiles to Jerusalem, it was like a dream! We were filled with laughter, and we sang for joy."*
> *(Psalm 126:1,2)*

"We couldn't help it, we were so happy." Peter says in his first letter,

> *"You love him even though you have never seen him. Though you do not see him now, you trust him; and you rejoice with a glorious, inexpressible joy." (1 Peter 1:8)*

Twice I've been in the company of Christians where the presence of the Lord has been so great they've laughed with a holy laughter in prayer.

I've been reading a remarkable book this last week about a man called Brother Andrew who pioneered the smuggling of Bibles into Eastern Europe. He gives the story of a particularly dangerous crossing, going across the Romanian border. He was waiting at the checkpoint. Six cars were in front of him waiting to go over. The inspection by the guards and soldiers was so thorough that they not only looked at all the baggage and took it all to pieces, but they actually removed the seats from the car and took the hubcaps from the wheels. They even stripped the engine of one car looking for anything that might be smuggled. Those six cars took four hours to get through. The car behind him was equally treated. But this particular car, which of course he had prayed over, full of Bibles, full of things for which he could be imprisoned for many years, if not executed, went through that frontier in 30 seconds. He'd actually prayed this prayer, "Lord, I will be depending utterly on you." And he records after passing the barrier these words: "My heart was racing, not with the excitement of the crossing but the excitement of having caught such a spectacular glimpse of God at work." He doesn't record that he laughed at that point, though other similar stories in that book say just that, but I'm quite certain at least he laughed and praised in his heart as he saw God at work like this.

But with Abraham, this was a laughter of faith. When God had given him this promise, there was still no proof whatsoever that the promise was going to be fulfilled. No sign, no evidence, no indication that God was really at work. But having seen that God was almighty and having believed again in his promise, he then laughed and praised.

"I waited patiently for the Lord to help me."
(Psalm 40:1)

I think a number of you have been waiting very patiently for the Lord in various ways, longing for the Lord to act. You want the Lord to reveal himself, to guide you, to answer some prayer, to heal you, whatever it may be, and you've been waiting very, very patiently for the Lord. Can we today learn this basic lesson from Abraham? We hear about the power of prayer. The power of praise is far greater. Abraham was 99, having had 24 years of disappointment, and he began to laugh and praise. Within a year the promised child was born.

Let us pray:
Abraham could be so happy in his God because he knew about this new relationship with him. If you are not clear about this in your own life, do ask God to show you, to reveal himself to you. And if you've been waiting on God for something, overcome the impatience or even bitterness by praising God for his power and faithfulness.

We thank you, Heavenly Father, that you are God Almighty, so great that you brought the whole universe into being. And so caring, you care about our tiny problems. Forgive us that we doubt you, we doubt your promises, we doubt your word. And Lord, give us all a new faith in you, a new vision of you, that we may in our lives go out laughing and praising in all your goodness and mercy. We ask this, Heavenly Father, for Jesus Christ's sake. Amen.

Knowing God by faith

> *"The LORD appeared again to Abraham near the oak grove belonging to Mamre. One day Abraham was sitting at the entrance to his tent during the hottest part of the day."*
> *(Genesis 18:1)*

I suppose I'm not one of the lucky ones because I don't seem to have the experiences of God or Christ that some people talk about. Often people say something like this to me when I talk to them about Christ. "The Lord said to me..." they claim. "The Lord spoke to me, the Lord came to me, the Lord appeared to me..." But I don't find that he does. So I don't suppose I'm one of the lucky ones. I wonder if you have ever felt the same?

Well, how does the Lord appear? What does it mean today when we cannot see him and we cannot touch him? How can we see him by faith? How can we touch him by faith? How can we listen to his voice today? They're very important questions. Often people say, "well I pray to God every day, every night." That's excellent. Of course we should talk to the Lord. But even more important, does he talk to us? Suppose you went to the doctor with some complaint and you talked all the time, and you left without the doctor saying a word, without giving you a prescription. It would be almost useless. Therefore I want to look at this slightly unusual passage in Genesis 18 more closely to see what it means to be in a place where the

Lord can actually come to you and speak to you and reveal himself to you. I want to look at the questions <u>When</u>? and <u>How</u>? and <u>What</u>?

First of all, <u>When</u> the Lord came. Notice verse 1 again, *"The LORD appeared again...Abraham was sitting at the entrance to his tent during the hottest part of the day"* In other words, he was having a siesta. He was quiet, he was thinking, he was resting, he was meditating. Nearly always, that is essential before you can hear the voice of God.

> *"Be still and know that I am God,"* *(Psalm 46:10).*

> *"Stand still and watch the Lord's victory."* *(2 Chronicles 20:17)*

> *"Wait here until I have received instructions for you from the Lord."* *(Numbers 9:8)*

> *"Pay attention to this, Job. Stop and consider the wonderful miracles of God!"* *(Job 37:14)*

These are some of the great commands in the Bible for you and I to be still before him. Otherwise we will never hear his voice. In a nutshell, I suppose that is the reason why comparatively few people - even Christians - hear the voice of the Lord, more than just once in a while. Because today we seem to find it very difficult to stay quiet and still in our minds and hearts. We very seldom meditate, and meditate carefully, on God's word. Isaiah says,

"In quietness and confidence is your strength."
(Isaiah 30:15)

An American missionary who was martyred in Ecuador, called Jim Elliot, made this comment on that verse; "I think the devil has made it his business to monopolise on three elements. The three main ways the devil attacks are these: noise, hurry, crowds. If he can keep us hearing radios, gossip, conversations, or even sermons, he is happy. But he will not allow quietness." I think this is shrewd, because most people seem to be bound by these three things: noise, hurry, and crowds.

You don't have to work in a large factory, to suffer from noise. You find noise wherever you go – out in the streets, in a café. You can turn on the television or radio in your own home. There is plenty of noise, and noise nearly always leads to tension. I was interested to read just a day or two ago that according to scientists, if you sleep in a room near busy traffic or near a railway line then, even if you never wake up, when something rattles past your window you suffer as much strain or tension as if you were holding a brick at arm's length for the same period of time. So you go to sleep, you wake up, and you're still tired; all because of noise. (Some of us may find we are still tired even if we don't have noise!) Nevertheless, today is certainly the age of noise and tension.

Again, it is also the age of speed and rush. Rush hour happens every day, maybe four times a day for some people. People rushing to the shops to and fro. Cars rushing to the coast - or queuing slowly to the coast. We have no time just to think. We have no time for anything. And many of us, I think, would rather envy that young lady in the famous limerick:

"There was a young lady named Bright,
Whose speed was far faster than light.
She set out one day, in a relative way,
And returned home the previous night."

This is indeed the age of speed and rush. It's also of course the age of crowds. Wherever you go, there are crowds. And in those crowds of course, you go on hearing the noise, and the conversation. "She said to me... and I said to her..." And it goes on and on and on. So it's very, very hard to be quiet in our own mind and heart, in our own being. Indeed, we sometimes find ourselves in a vicious circle. It seems that people want noise and rush and crowds because without them they feel insecure. You see, when you are very quiet, and you think about the world, it seems a very frightening place. When you are very quiet and thinking about your own situation, it may seem very grim. Yet the very noise and rush and crowds, that people seem to want, merely increase the tension and in fact make them less secure, like never before. Therefore, God says,

"Be still and know that I am God."
(Psalm 46:10)

I believe Emerson, the 19th century American orator and philosopher, once rushed out of a committee meeting where they had been having a very heated discussion and argument. He was feeling very hot and flushed and angry and impatient. He went out into the evening, into the open, and he looked up into the stars. The stars seemed to say to him, "Why so hot, little man? Why so hot, little man? Look at the greatness of God! Look at his majesty! Look at his handiwork! Now, what about your problem? Why so hot, little man? Be still and know that I am God."

The story of Mary and Martha was recorded precisely to show this point. Mary was sitting quietly at the feet of Jesus, quiet in her whole being, listening to his voice, listening to his teaching. Martha, on the other hand, was dashing around to and fro, anxious and troubled about many things – the word that is used is "distracted". The actual word is one you might use to describe a busy street. Her thoughts were dashing here, dashing there, dashing everywhere. She had a crowd within her – her crowded thoughts.

I believe this idea of stillness and quietness is particularly a problem for those of you who know that by nature you are a practical sort of person. You always like to be up and doing; you don't like to be sitting down, being quiet. And I think sometimes a person who is a practical sort of person finds it very hard to be still in God's presence and to think, to meditate. Well, unless you are still, you'll never hear the voice of the Lord. Remember how Jesus said, *"When you pray, go into your room and shut the door"?* (Matt 6:6). In one sense this is precisely what we have to do wherever we are, whether we are at home or not. We are to go into our room, and shut the door on outside things, shut the door on all that we're doing, shut the door on our housework, on our job, on our family, and shut ourselves in with God alone.

"Be still and know that I am God."

Otherwise we shall never have a deep experience of Christ, we shall never hear his voice. We will not know what he is saying to us.

In passing, it's just worth noticing here that Abraham was sitting at the door of his tent *"during the hottest part of the day"* and, although I don't think you can read too much into those words, in other places in the Bible they are used to describe a time of trial and oppression or affliction. Therefore I think we may sometimes find that unless we learn this quietness the easy way, God may have to allow suffering or affliction or sickness, so that we simply have to be quiet and have to listen to his voice. Certainly, very often the "heat of the day" – a time of pressure – could be and can be a time of spiritual blessing if we learn to use it like that. There's the first thing then

- <u>when</u> the Lord came. When Abraham was quiet in his heart.

Secondly, I'd like to talk about <u>how</u> the Lord appeared.

> *"He looked up and noticed three men standing nearby. When he saw them, he ran to meet them and welcomed them, bowing low to the ground." (Genesis 18:2)*

Who were these men? Well, I'll give you the answer and then we'll look at the verses. They were in fact the Lord and two angels. If you find that very puzzling, then look on a little bit further, to verse 9. See here the three men who said to him,

> *"'Where is Sarah your wife?' the visitors asked. 'She's inside the tent.'... Then the Lord said...'"*

You see, one of the three was the Lord. And then go on to verse 22,

> *"The other men turned and headed toward Sodom, but the LORD remained with Abraham..."*

In other words, two of the men went off leaving Abraham with the Lord, the third man. Then chapter 19 verse 1 says, *"That evening the two*

angels came to the entrance of the city of Sodom" —
these were the two that had gone off.

So a simple piece of detective work shows us here that the three men were in fact the Lord and two angels. Now that may seem very strange, since Paul said that no man has seen God at any time. (I Timothy 6:16) But you will find that there are certain places in the Old Testament where Christ appeared to people before his incarnation. This is one of them. I needn't worry you too much about that sort of theological detail. What is the relevance of this as far as we are concerned? I think the relevance is this: that the Lord appeared to Abraham almost in disguise. He scarcely realised that it was the Lord — just one of three men. Indeed, had not Abraham been quiet in his own heart, and thinking and alert for the Lord, he might have missed him altogether. He might never have heard his voice or his message. In a slightly different way, perhaps today we need to be alert to the various different ways the Lord may appear to us. It's so easy to be spiritually blind or deaf. We open our Bibles and it's just a book. We come to a service and it's just a preacher. We talk to a Christian and oh, it's just Tom, it's Jane. We read a Christian book — it's just a story. But if we are alert, looking for the Lord and really listening for him, many, many times, you won't find it is just a book, it's just the Bible, it's just a preacher, it's just a Christian, you will find it is the Lord himself.

Every Sunday I pray for some time that during the services the Lord himself might speak through some part of the service, maybe through the sermon. I believe that many people have heard the voice of God in this way. Oh, you may hear my words coming from my own physical lips, but in the quietness of your heart, you know that in fact it is God speaking to you. I may have no idea at all that he is doing it. But in your heart something is saying, "that's for me, that message is for me". I think you will nearly always hear the voice of the Lord whenever you come to a service like this, whenever you open your Bible, whenever you are talking about Christ, and if you are looking for him, seeking him, listening for his voice. I think that every single time you will be blessed. Sometimes we come in a sleepy frame of mind or a critical frame of mind or just not expecting anything very much. But if you come looking for the Lord, I am quite certain he will bless you. Indeed of course he could speak to you, as he has often spoken to me, through people, even through a non-Christian. Sometimes a challenge, or a rebuke. Some of you will know this verse.

"Not only in the words you say,
Not only in your deeds confessed,
But in the most unconscious way,
Is Christ expressed.

"For me, 'twas not the truth you taught,
To you so clear to me so dim.
But when you came to me you brought,
A sense of him.

"And from your eyes, He beckons me,
And from your heart his love is shed,
'Till I lose sight of you and see
The living Christ instead."

(Portrait of a Christian by Beatrice Clelland)

Often that poem is quoted to show the value and power of Christian witness. But perhaps even more important, the writer was sensitive and alert for the Lord to show her something. So she could see the Lord and hear the Lord and feel the Lord's love in another Christian, because she was looking. So that's when the Lord came and how the Lord appeared. And thirdly what the Lord found. In this story he found two things: Abraham's eagerness and Sarah's unbelief. Firstly Abraham's eagerness: you see this in a very delightful way here at the end of verse 2,

> *"When he saw them, he ran to meet them and welcomed them, bowing low to the ground..."*

And verses 6 & 7,

> *"So Abraham ran back to the tent and said to Sarah, "Hurry! Get three large measures of your best flour, knead it into dough, and bake some bread." Then Abraham ran out to the herd and chose a tender calf and gave it to his servant, who quickly prepared it."*

A man aged one hundred! He was pretty eager, very eager indeed. Now you could say this was just an Eastern custom. Yes, but it's a very good custom. I think today the motto of many is that "I keep myself to myself." We don't readily open our hearts; we don't even open our doors to anybody except perhaps our family or our immediate circle of friends. But the Bible says that for the Christian it ought to be very different.

> "Don't forget to show hospitality to strangers, for some who have done this have entertained angels without realizing it!" (Hebrews 13:2)

Here Abraham was entertaining not only angels but the Lord himself. As Matthew 25 verse 34 reminds us, one day, on the Judgment Day, Christ is going to separate everybody onto one side and the other side. And he'll say to one,

> "Come, you who are blessed by my Father, inherit the Kingdom prepared for you from the creation of the world."

And he'll go on to say why,

> "For I was hungry, and you fed me. I was thirsty, and you gave me a drink. I was a stranger, and you invited me into your home ..." (Matt 25:34-36)

And they will say, "When, we don't remember that?"

> "When you did it to one of the least of these my brothers and sisters, you were doing it to me."

And to others he will say,

> "Away with you, you cursed ones, into the eternal fire prepared for the devil and his demons. For I was hungry, and you didn't feed me. I was thirsty, and you didn't give me a drink. I was a stranger, and you didn't invite me into your home."

"Lord, when? We don't remember that. We'd have done it if you were there."

> "when you refused to help the least of these my brothers and sisters, you were refusing to help me".

If we claim to follow the Lord and love him, our hearts should be large towards other people. We should care for their needs; we should open our doors to other people who may indeed need help. I do believe we need to learn much more about this hospitality. If the gospel is going to go forward in this city and this country, it's got to use people's homes. And I hope that your door will be an open door for many people. Be eager to show hospitality. Certainly when it comes to fellowship with the Lord himself, we need the same form of eagerness, because in his love God will never force himself on anyone.

In verse 3 Abraham says,

> "My lord," he said, "if it pleases you, stop here for a while."

He went out and said, "Lord, come in! I want you to come in." In the same way, the risen Christ went with those two disciples on the road to Emmaus and he walked with them, and we are told that they drew near to the village to which they were going. He appeared to be going farther, he wasn't going to force himself upon them. But they said,

> "Stay the night with us, since it is getting late." (Luke 24:29)

If you really want Jesus, if you really want him to speak, if you really want him to reveal his will for you day by day, quite certainly he will. "Seek and you will find." If you don't seek, you won't find. If you don't listen, you won't hear.

Then Sarah's unbelief, in verse 9:

> "'Where is Sarah, your wife?' the visitors asked 'She's inside the tent,' Abraham replied."

The Lord said (renewing his promise, remember),

>*"I will return to you about this time next year, and your wife, Sarah, will have a son!"*

Sarah was listening to all that was going on. It says here that Sarah *"was listening to this conversation from the tent"*. *(Genesis 18:10)* It goes on to say in verse 12 that *"she laughed silently to herself"*. "What nonsense! What nonsense! Ridiculous! I'm an old person. Of course I won't have a son," she thought to herself. As she went on listening, suddenly she could have been knocked over with a feather because the Lord said,

>*"Why did Sarah laugh? Why did she say, 'Can an old woman like me have a baby?'"*

As she listened, Sarah was now trembling because she realised that this was a divine guest who knew her very thoughts, even the secrets in her heart. So she said, trying to hide it, "Well, I-I-I didn't laugh." She was afraid, the Bible says. The Lord replied, "no, you <u>did</u> laugh."

I want you to see, from this last point why the Lord came. Clearly Sarah was convicted at that moment. He came because he cared. In Hebrews 11 the writer says that <u>by faith</u> Sarah received power to conceive. She would never have conceived a child, Isaac would never have been born, if she had continued in unbelief. So the Lord came to her because he cared. And the Lord convicted her of her unbelief. No doubt she confessed it later. The Lord gave her a gift of faith, and by faith she conceived.

He came because he cared. That's always the reason why he comes. Whether he encourages you or comforts you, or rebukes you, or convicts you, he comes because he cares. I trust that you and I will learn this inner silence in a world that is so full of noise and bustle and crowds. And I trust that we shall be looking for the Lord and listening for him day by day. Jesus said,

> *"God blesses those whose hearts are pure."*
> *(Matthew 5:8)*

The person with a pure heart is not only someone with clean thoughts; he is somebody whose heart is single. He is looking for the Lord, he is listening for the Lord, he is searching for the Lord in all he does, day by day. As he opens his Bible, as he walks down the street, as he talks to people, he is looking for the Lord. Jesus said, "that person will see God" over and over again. I trust we will be such people, who will see the Lord like that. Then when we find him and listen to him again and again and again, we'll see how much he cares.

The secret things of God

> "Should I hide my plan from Abraham?" the
> LORD asked... I have singled him out so that
> he will direct his sons and their families to keep
> the way of the LORD by doing what is right and
> just. Then I will do for Abraham all that I have
> promised" (Genesis 18:17,19)

Most people love secrets. It is often said that if you
want to spread a story as fast as possible, then you
tell it to someone in confidence. "Just between
you and me... Don't tell a soul." And that story will
go around like lightning. Most people love secrets.
It actually says in Proverbs that the words of a
whisperer are like delicious morsels (Proverbs
18:8). They just slip down inside us because we
love secrets.

However, some secrets really bring with them a
great sense of responsibility. For example, if I
discovered the secret formula to cure cancer, I
would have a most urgent duty to pass that
formula on. If I discovered a secret plot to
assassinate the Prime Minister I think I would have
an urgent duty to pass that secret on. Scientists
often have very great trouble when they realise
the moral consequences of some discovery. I'm
told that the first person who discovered the
potential power of the atom spent the rest of his
life campaigning for peace.

Of course in the spiritual realm there are great secrets which bring great responsibilities. In Deuteronomy chapter 29 and verse 29 it says,

> "The LORD our God has secrets known to no one. We are not accountable for them, but we and our children are accountable forever for all that he has revealed to us, so that we may obey all the terms of these instructions."

Because God in his love has revealed to us many secrets – about himself, about the world, about ourselves – it is essential, if we know those secrets, to do something about them. For example, countless people all around are thirsty for a life which satisfies. They try desperately to find it in drink, drugs, sex, marriage, money, whatever it may be, and still they are dissatisfied. Jesus said,

> "Anyone who is thirsty may come to me!"
> (John 7:37)
>
> "But those who drink the water I give will never be thirsty again" (John 4:14)

Many people have problems and anxieties and burdens. Prescriptions for antidepressants continue to rise each year. Jesus said,

> *"Come to me, all of you who are weary and carry heavy burdens, and I will give you rest."* (Matthew 11:28)

The vast majority of people believe they have no purpose in life, and don't know where they are going. Jesus said,

> *"I am the way"* (John 14:6)

> *"I am the light of the world. If you follow me, you won't have to walk in darkness, because you will have the light that leads to life."* (John 8:12)

When it comes to death, Jesus told us many times there is a judgment to come, that he died to save us from the judgment, but that without him we have no hope whatsoever.

Now many of us know these things, many of us have received Christ as our saviour. We know that we are forgiven. We know that we have peace with God. We know that in Christ we are going to heaven. We know these things. These are the secret things of God revealed to us; they belong to us, they are ours. And with them come great responsibilities.

> *"Should I hide my plan from Abraham?"*

So, in this story, what was it that God determined not to hide from Abraham? Well, it was his impending judgment on that godless city of Sodom. In verse 20 he describes the city,

> *"I have heard a great outcry from Sodom and Gomorrah, because their sin is so flagrant."*

And so that city was about to be destroyed.

Now why do you think that God revealed this secret to Abraham? Was it that Abraham might be thankful in his own heart that he was not condemned? Was it that Abraham might come to church every Sunday and praise God for all his blessings? Oh no. The church today is crippled because far too many Christians remain at the receiving end. Perhaps they wander from church to church, tasting sermons. Providing they go to church somewhere they think that God will be pleased.

Now, I don't want you to misunderstand me here, I think that it is right sometimes for a person to seek a church which is fairly alive spiritually, because without that you may not be able to receive the word of the Lord, without it you may not be able to offer very much. But there is a real danger in adopting this kind of attitude: "providing I am getting helped, providing I am receiving some comfort, that's all that matters". Is it? Why does God give us spiritual help? Why does he reveal himself to us? Jesus said,

> *"When someone has been given much, much will be required in return."* (Luke 12:48)

Without any doubt at all, very much has been given to all of us in churches up and down this country. We have freedom of worship, and we have freedom of fellowship. There are thousands of Christians elsewhere in the world today who would literally be risking their lives to come to a service like the ones we enjoy. Maybe some of them would be captured and spend the rest of their lives in prison. We have freedom to witness. You can talk to a person about Jesus without risking losing your job, without risking going to prison; thousands can't. I would urge you, if you go to a church fairly regularly, to get involved, to get stuck in, to become an active member of the Body of Christ. Too often the Body of Christ is a paralyzed body. It lurches forward in a clumsy, horrible way, making no progress.

One of the great chapters of the New Testament is John chapter 15 where Jesus says,

> *"I have told you these things so that you will be filled with my joy. Yes, your joy will overflow!"*

> *"You didn't choose me. I chose you."*

He goes on to explain why he chose us:

> *"...to go and produce lasting fruit."*

There's a work for Jesus only you can do. That's what God was saying to Abraham here.

"Should I hide my plan from Abraham?"

God told Abraham of the coming judgment upon Sodom for two very good reasons. Firstly, that he might later instruct his children and household about the ways of the Lord. You see that in verse 19:

> *"I have singled him out so that he will direct his sons and their families to keep the way of the LORD by doing what is right and just."*

What a responsibility! Yet surely here is a work for Jesus which no-one can do but you. Because if you are not active in trying to help your family and your circle of friends and those immediately around you, who else will do it? No-one else has the same circle of friends and family, no-one else at all. You have that solemn responsibility. If God has shown you something of the truth of himself - that he is a God of love and holiness, that he brings salvation but that there is judgment, that Christ is the only way to God and to heaven - then surely you must do all you possibly can to make your own circle of friends and relations know something about it. It's not always easy, but if you're a parent I trust that you are praying for your children, that you say grace at meals, that you have family prayers if you can. If you're a young person, you can't preach at your parents. But you can pray for them, you can live as a Christian in front of them. You can lend Christian books, bring them along to a service. The same applies to a Christian husband with a non-Christian wife and vice versa.

Some of you remember the woman who wrote to Gypsy Smith[3] after a mission and said, "I've come to Jesus Christ during the mission. I feel that God is calling me to preach the gospel. The trouble is I've got 12 children." The reply was, "I'm very glad God has called you. I'm glad you've been given a congregation too."

You see, you and I often have a mission in our homes, in our streets, in the area where we live and work. Why not make your house - whether it's a large one or a small one - a house church? Call in your friends and neighbours. Play a tape, maybe of an evangelistic service, or ask someone to come and to give a short word. I believe if everyone who could do this actually did it, and did it regularly, the total impact on this city and the surrounding area would be immense. I'm convinced of it. Far more than the impact of just one church, people coming to just one building.

"Shall I hide from you the gospel of Christ?" God may say to us today. "And the judgment to come, shall I hide this from you? No I won't, because I have chosen you and I want you to go out and bring forth fruit. I want you to tell your friends and family and neighbours." If you don't, who will?

---

[3] Rodney 'Gypsy' Smith, 1860-1947, British evangelist.

That's the first reason why God revealed his purpose to Abraham in this story.

The second reason is this: that he might pray immediately for the people of Sodom, that the judgment of God might not fall. You see there is nothing arbitrary about God's judgment. Let me put it like this. If I put my hand in the fire, it will get burnt. Obvious. If I run out in front of a fast-moving car, I will get run over. If I go on breaking God's commandments, I'll be punished. It's obvious; I bring it upon myself. It's my own fault.

However, God has given us a secret weapon by which, if you and I use it, we can stop God's hand of judgment coming upon a person, coming upon a city, coming upon even a nation. And that is the power of intercessory prayer. Don't ask me about how it works. I can't tell you. All I know is it works. Read the story of Moses, how time and time again God's judgment was about to fall and Moses prayed. The people escaped the judgment of God. Read the stories of Samuel and Job and Isaiah and Ezekiel and Jeremiah and Paul and many, many more. Read the stories today of the power of prayer. I've often found that on the receiving end, during missions or during guest services, there is special power there because there is somebody, or may be several people, really praying. Men, women, and young people are brought to Jesus Christ. It's the only reason.

One person found that again and again God was using him to win people for Christ, and whenever

76

he preached people seemed to be gripped by what he was saying. As he was preaching one particular evening and people were listening most attentively, he saw a vision: heaven opened and light streamed down from heaven – not upon himself, but upon his poor, blind brother praying in the front pew. It was through that intercessory prayer of his brother – that no-one really thought about, no-one really knew – that God was at work. And I have no doubt that if you know something of God's truth and the need of those who are without him, you have a great responsibility to pray. Not just for yourselves, but for those who are in danger of God's judgment.

In closing, let's look very briefly at Abraham's prayer for Sodom here in this chapter. We see he was confident. In verses 22 and 23 he stood before the Lord and he drew near, because by faith he knew that he was right with God, and if you have a personal faith in Jesus Christ, all the time you have an open door into God's presence. You can come with confidence. He was reverent (verse 27). He said,

> "Since I have begun, let me speak further to my Lord, even though I am but dust and ashes."

He didn't abuse the privilege of prayer. He didn't treat God as his pal or his servant. He knew that he had no right to come into God's presence at all. As a sinner, he had no right to ask for anything.

Sometimes people today pray as though they had a right to ask God for everything, as though God were there to serve them. But Abraham was fervent. Look at verse 23 and then verse 25.

> "Abraham approached him and said, 'Will you sweep away both the righteous and the wicked?'"

> "Surely you wouldn't do such a thing, destroying the righteous along with the wicked. Why, you would be treating the righteous and the wicked exactly the same! Surely you wouldn't do that! Should not the Judge of all the earth do what is right?"

He was fervent in his prayer: "Lord, you can't do this. You're the judge of all the earth. You can't destroy righteous people." James 5:16 says,

> "The earnest prayer of a righteous person has great power and produces wonderful results."

There was no vagueness about his prayer, it wasn't a "Lord, bless everyone everywhere" type of prayer. It was definite, because his prayer was based upon facts. He knew the character of God, that God was a holy God and a loving God. He knew that Sodom was a wicked city and that judgment must come. But he knew that God was just, and would not destroy the righteous. Because he knew these things he prayed a bold, definite,

78

believing prayer. That is always the secret of powerful prayer. It is based on facts about God, his word, and his promises.

Above all, Abraham was persevering. In his prayer, Abraham went on and on pleading no less than six times with God. "Oh God," he said "you're in charge of all the earth. You won't destroy the righteous. God, supposing there are only 50 people in this city, won't you spare the city?" "Yes," says God, "I will for 50." And Abraham thinks maybe there aren't 50, but there could be 45. "Lord, if there are only 45, will you spare it?" "Yes, for 45." "Lord, if there are only 40, will you spare it?" "Yes, for 40." "Lord, supposing there are only 30?" "Yes, for 30." "Or only 20?" "Yes, for 20." "Lord, supposing there are only ten?" "Yes," said God, "even for ten, I will spare that city." Abraham is persevering, going on, pleading, arguing with God.

Yet the end of the story is tragic. Because in spite of Abraham's prayer, that city was utterly destroyed. Why? The answer is most important: because Abraham made a false and serious assumption. As he pleaded with God for even ten people, he was thinking of one particular family – his nephew Lot, Mrs Lot, their two sons, their four daughters and their two sons-in-law. Ten all together. He knew that Lot was righteous – and the New Testament confirms that Lot was righteous (2 Peter 2:7) – but he made a great mistake because he assumed (as many do today) that because Lot was righteous, his family were also righteous. But God's salvation is always individual. Every individual must come and put their trust in Jesus Christ. It's no good anyone saying, "well, I come from a Christian family. My parents are Christian, my brother's a Christian, my sister's a Christian. My husband's a Christian, my wife's a Christian." Every person must come to Jesus Christ. In Lot's family it turned out that his sons were quite indifferent. His sons-in-law and their wives refused to listen, and even his own wife turned back and perished. Only two unmarried daughters escaped with Lot. Not even ten righteous persons in that city. Lot escaped because of Abraham's prayer, but Sodom itself was destroyed. If only Abraham had gone further on with his persevering prayer.

Samuel once said to the people,

> "As for me, I will certainly not sin against the LORD by ending my prayers for you."
> (1 Samuel 12:23)

Now I'm quite sure that many of us know something about the secrets of God and his word. You know about salvation, you know about judgment. You have come to know Jesus for yourself. If you haven't, or you're not sure, I hope you will talk to someone right now about this very thing. But if God has revealed to you the truth about the need of those near you, around you, perhaps in your own home, who are without Christ, then you have tremendous responsibilities.

I trust that by praying and by speaking, you will do all that you possibly can, with the help of the Lord, to make people see their need of Jesus Christ. God forbid that any of our friends should miss God's salvation through our own fault.

Let us pray:
   Perhaps you know in your heart that there is a member of your family, or a next-door neighbour, someone you often see, who knows nothing of forgiveness in Christ. Ask God now to give you a burden, a concern, a love for them.
   If Christ is still a real stranger to you, ask him to show himself as a friend and a saviour who longs to enter your life.

   Heavenly Father, we thank you that we have been given much by you. We thank you for the gospel, for our salvation, for the Bible and freedom of worship. We know that many people do not know about Jesus. Take complacency away from us, take away the expectation that we just receive from you, but not give. Father, help us to face up to our responsibilities, so that it may be our desire to win our friends for Jesus. We ask it for his glorious sake. Amen.